Living in Groups

Julie Haydon

Chapter 1
Living in Groups

Many animals live in groups. Some animals live in groups all of their lives, and other animals live in groups for just part of their lives.

Animal groups range from small to large.

Group living has many **advantages**. In a group, it can be easier to:

- 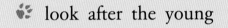 find food and water
- kill **prey**
- watch for enemies
- fight or scare off enemies
- look after the young
- build a home
- keep warm

These birds are building a home.

Chapter 2
A Herd of Elephants

Elephants live in family groups called herds. A herd is made up of female elephants, young male elephants, and baby elephants. Older male elephants will join a herd for a short time when it is time to **mate** with a female.

Problem

Healthy adult elephants are so large and strong that they do not need to fear other animals, except humans. However baby elephants can be killed by **predators**, such as lions. Baby elephants can also get stuck in mud and drown in rivers.

5

Solution

All the female elephants in a herd watch over the baby elephants. If a predator **threatens** a baby elephant, the females will surround the baby and keep it safe. If a baby elephant gets into trouble in water or mud, a female will help the baby get free.

Other Advantages

An elephant herd is led by the oldest female elephant. She has learned where the water holes and best places to find food are.

Chapter 3
A Pack of Wolves

Wolves live in packs. Each wolf knows its place in the pack. A male wolf and a female wolf usually lead a pack. They are called the alpha pair. The alpha pair eat first and often lead attacks on enemies. The alpha pair often mate and have pups.

Problem

A wolf needs to eat a lot of meat. A wolf on its own cannot catch and kill large animals, such as deer and moose. A single wolf is also in danger of being attacked by animals, such as cougars and bears.

Solution

Wolves work as a team, so they can hunt and kill large animals. Wolves also protect their **territory** and their pups from other animals.

Other Advantages

When a female wolf has pups, the other wolves bring her food. All the wolves in a pack help to train and look after the pups.

Chapter 4
A School of Fish

Many fish swim in large groups called schools. All the fish in a school swim very closely together. When one fish moves, all the other fish follow. This happens so quickly that the school can look like it is one large animal.

Problem

If a predator, such as a shark, sees a fish swimming on its own in the open ocean, the fish is in real danger. The predator may attack and take the fish by surprise. Even if the fish sees the predator, it has nowhere to hide.

Solution

Many fish swim in schools. This way there are lots of fish to look out for danger. If a predator sees the school, it is hard for the predator to pick one fish out of the group to eat.

Other Advantages

Fish that live in schools have a good chance of finding a mate because there are so many fish to choose from. Fish in schools all help to find food.

Chapter 5
A Flock of Geese

In autumn many geese fly from their **breeding grounds** to a warmer place where there is plenty of food. After winter the birds fly back to the breeding grounds. This happens every year and is called **migration**. Migrating geese often flock together and fly in the shape of a V.

Problem

A migrating goose has a long way to fly. Flying is hard work, and it uses up a lot of energy. A goose on its own must flap its wings often to move through the air.

Solution

The geese in a flock take turns flying at the front of the V. The lead bird has to work the hardest. As it flies, it moves the air. This helps the birds behind the leader have a smoother flight. They can even glide some of the way. This uses less energy.

Other Advantages

When geese fly in a V-shape, they can **communicate** with each other. When the geese land to eat, several geese look out for danger. If they see or hear an enemy, they call out loudly.

Chapter 6
Snakes in a Den

Snakes are **cold-blooded** animals. They lie, or bask, in the sun to get warm. Some snakes, such as these garter snakes, will spend time in large groups.

Problem

Snakes cannot make their own body heat, yet some garter
snakes live in places with very cold winters.

Solution

During winter garter snakes **hibernate** in large groups in dens. This helps the snakes to stay warm. In spring the garter snakes come out of their dens.

Other Advantages

In spring the male garter snakes come out of the den first. They wait for the females to leave the den, hoping to find a mate.

Chapter 7
A Herd of Zebras

Some zebras live in herds. A herd is made up of female zebras and their young and a male zebra. The male zebra, a stallion, leads the herd.

Problem

A zebra on its own is in danger of being killed by a predator, such as a lion. A single zebra is also easy to see because of its stripes.

Solution

In a herd, there are lots of zebras to watch and listen for danger. When zebras are together, their stripes make it hard to tell one animal from another. This can confuse predators and give the zebras time to escape.

Other Advantages

A stallion will try to protect the female zebras and babies in his herd. The stallion has a powerful kick and can hurt or kill a predator.

Chapter 8
Animal Groups

How does living in a group help these animals?

a swarm of honeybees

a school of dolphins